Pullout Poster Instructions

Before tearing out each poster, fold back and forth along the perforations several times. Tear out each poster slowly and carefully. Place your thumb at the top of the poster next to the perforations. With your other hand, tear along the perforations, moving your thumb down as you go.

Cover photographs, front and back, ©2003 CIA Stock Photography, Inc., except for Kevin Harvick photograph ©2003 Action Sports Photography, Inc.

CE

Copyright © 2004 NASCAR and Reader's Digest Children's Publishing, Inc.
Published by Reader's Digest Children's Books, Reader's Digest Road, Pleasantville, NY U.S.A. 10570-7000
and Reader's Digest Children's Publishing Limited, The Ice House, 124-126 Walcot Street, Bath UK BA1 5BG
Reader's Digest Children's Books is a trademark and Reader's Digest is a registered trademark of The Reader's Digest Association, Inc.
NASCAR® is a registered trademark of the National Association for Stock Car Auto Racing, Inc.
Roush Racing and Matt Kenseth's name and likeness used by authority of Roush Racing, Livonia, MI.
The yellow/black color scheme is a trademark of DEWALT® Power Tools and accessories.
"Bobby Labonte®," "#18®", and "Interstate® Batteries" licensed under authority of Joe Gibbs Racing, Huntersville, NC.
Penske Racing South, Inc. trademarks, including the #12 and the likeness of the race car, and Ryan Newman's name and/or likeness are granted by license from Penske Racing South, Inc. ALLTEL marks are registered trademarks of ALLTEL Corp.
The Stylized "29", the likeness of the Number 29 Race Car and the RCR Checkered Flag Logo are Trademarks of RCR Enterprises, LLC, and are used under license from RCR Enterprises, LLC. The name, likeness and signature of Kevin Harvick are trademarks of Kevin Harvick, Incorporated, and are used under license from Kevin Harvick, Incorporated.
The trademarks "Goodwrench" and "GM" are used under license from General Motors Corporation.
All rights reserved. Manufactured in China. Conforms to ASTM F963
10 9 8 7 6 5 4 3 2

Hittin' the Road

Hittin' the Road

Most NASCAR races are held at oval tracks where drivers make only left turns. Twice during the season, however, racers head to "road courses." On these twisty tracks, drivers must turn left, right, and sometimes make wide U-turns as the courses weave over the landscape. Road courses test a driver's steering, braking, and gear-shifting skills. The key is finding the right "line" through all the curves, and staying on that line to maintain the highest possible speed.

The two road courses are Infineon Raceway in California, and Watkins Glen in New York.

Poster photograph: ©2003 Action Sports Photography, Inc.

Heavy Traffic!

Heavy Traffic!

With 43 cars in a tight space during every race, NASCAR drivers must always be aware of the traffic around them. Moving around corners and down straightaways at nearly 200 miles per hour, they might be only inches away from an opponent. Drivers learn to trust each other's skills to avoid any problems, and rookie drivers quickly learn how to fit into the pack. NASCAR driving rules help prevent trouble, but every NASCAR driver knows that a little bumpin' is part of the game!

Poster photograph: ©2003 Action Sports Photography, Inc.

NASCAR

Matt Kenseth

17

Matt Kenseth

In 2003, Matt recorded only one victory (Las Vegas) but his many high finishes helped him capture his first overall NASCAR championship. The 2000 NASCAR Rookie of the Year posted 11 top-5 and 25 top-10 finishes in his drive to the title. The title didn't come easy for Matt. Dale Earnhardt Jr., Jeff Gordon, and Ryan Newman kept up the pressure throughout the year. After finishing 33rd and 36th in two races in September 2003, Matt asked 2002 NASCAR champion Tony Stewart for advice. The pep talk paid off for Matt and he never looked back.

17

Poster photograph: ©2003 CIA Stock Photography, Inc.

Matt Kenseth

Matt, who grew up in Cambridge, Wisconsin, didn't take up racing until the age of 16. But he was a natural at the sport and quickly became a racing superstar in the state. Robbie Reiser, Matt's current crew chief, saw potential in Matt and asked him to race for his NASCAR team.

In 2000, Matt and Robbie teamed up with Roush Racing to shock the racing world with a victory and 11 top-10 finishes as a rookie on the NASCAR Cup Series. In 2002, Matt led the NASCAR Cup Series with five victories, and he finished eighth in the overall points standings.

17

Poster photograph: ©2003 CIA Stock Photography, Inc.

Kevin Harvick

Kevin's youth has served him well in his NASCAR career. His fearless attitude and self-confidence reminded many people of the legendary Dale Earnhardt. In fact, in 2001 at age 25, Kevin took over the driving duties for the No. 29 car on the Richard Childress Racing team. Kevin lived up to the high hopes people had for him. While he continued to race in NASCAR's #2-rated series, he also won his third NASCAR Series race. Kevin won the overall title in the series below the NASCAR NEXTEL Cup Series and was named the NASCAR Raybestos Rookie of the Year.

Poster photograph: ©2004 Action Sports Photography, Inc.
Kevin Harvick photograph: ©2003 Sherryl Creekmore/NASCAR

Kevin Harvick

Kevin's nickname is "Happy," but don't let his boyish looks and friendliness fool you. He is a fierce competitor behind the wheel, as Jeff Gordon discovered in 2001. Kevin won his first NASCAR Cup Series race by defeating Gordon in an amazing last-lap finish at the Cracker Barrel 500 in Atlanta.

After his Rookie of the Year season, Kevin won in 2002 at Chicagoland Speedway for the second time. In 2003, he became the first driver in the ten-year history of the Brickyard race in Indianapolis to win from the pole. He finished fifth in the overall points standings.

Poster photograph: ©2003 Action Sports Photography, Inc.

Ryan Newman

Ryan's rise to NASCAR prominence hasn't just been fast—it's been meteoric! After winning more than 100 quarter-midget racing events, Ryan drove stock cars for the first time in 2000 and won in just his second race.

In 2002, he joined NASCAR's elite circuit and finished the year by winning the New Hampshire 300, capturing six pole positions, and collecting 14 top-5 finishes in 36 starts. All of his successes earned him 2002 NASCAR Rookie of the Year honors.

Poster photograph: ©2003 CIA Stock Photography, Inc.
Ryan Newman photograph: ©2003 Sherryl Creekmore/NASCAR

Ryan Newman

On the track and in the garage, Ryan uses lessons he learned in school. He has a vehicle structure engineering degree from Purdue University. He also has the driving skills to aim for victory lane many more times during his career.

The South Bend, Indiana, native had a sensational second NASCAR season in 2003. He led the series with eight victories and 17 top-fives. He earned 11 qualifying poles, tying him for second-most ever in a single season. Ryan finished sixth overall in the 2003 standings.

Poster photograph: ©2003 CIA Stock Photography, Inc.

NASCAR

Bobby Labonte

Bobby Labonte

Bobby had a great season in 2001, winning his first NASCAR title. With the victory, Bobby earned more than $4 million. He and Terry Labonte (1984 and 1996 champ) are the only brothers to both win NASCAR championships.

The owner of Bobby's car is Joe Gibbs, who won three Super Bowls as head coach of football's Washington Redskins. Bobby's 2001 season was marked by consistent excellence—he finished every race—and determination. Both are traits also fostered in football players coached by Gibbs.

Poster photograph: ©2003 CIA Stock Photography, Inc.

Bobby Labonte

Bobby Labonte

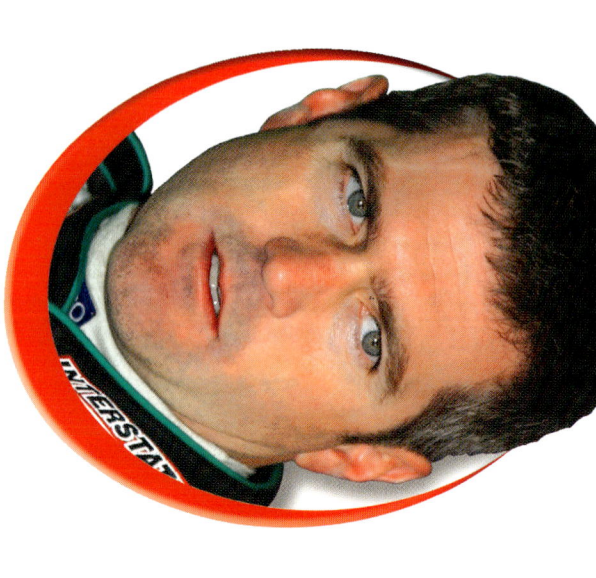

Bobby is a native of Corpus Christi, Texas, and began racing at age 5. When the Labonte family moved to North Carolina in 1979 to help Terry, who was a rising NASCAR star, Bobby thought his racing career would have to take a back seat to Terry's.

However, Bobby got a job working for Terry's racing team and helped his older brother win the NASCAR championship in 1984. Bobby's first NASCAR victory came at the Coca-Cola 600 in 1995. He has won at least one race in every season since then.

18

Poster photograph: ©2003 CIA Stock Photography, Inc.
Bobby Labonte photograph: ©2003 Sherryl Creekmore/NASCAR

Taking it to the Bank!

At more than 3,500 pounds, NASCAR race cars battle with the forces of physics in every race. As they head into turns, the weight of the car propels it in a straight path, while the drivers want the cars to turn left. Helping the drivers in their battle are "banks" like this one. In the corners of most tracks, the surface is at a steep angle. This reduces the pull of the weight of the car and helps make it a bit easier to steer around curves. High banks mean cars can keep their speed up, making for faster and more exciting races for fans.

Poster photograph: ©2003 CIA Stock Photography, Inc.

First to the Finish

Finding the "groove" in NASCAR means determining the best route around a racetrack. Every second counts and racers are always looking for the most efficient and quickest way to the finish line.

The groove changes depending on the track and the weather. The "high groove" takes a car closer to the outside wall for most of a lap. The "low groove" is found near the track's apron (closest to the infield). In 2000, driver Bobby Labonte (green car) found the groove more often than any other driver and captured the NASCAR championship.

Poster photograph: ©2003 Action Sports Photography, Inc.

Pit Stop!

Pit Stop!

NASCAR has a lot of brilliant drivers, so the difference between winning and losing can often be found in the pits. Every second counts in a race. A good pit stop can take as little as 15 seconds. If the pit crew is completing a four-tire stop, a good time is about 22 seconds.

Pit crews fill the race car with gas and change two or four tires. Other tasks include: repairing the body of the car, fixing broken parts, cleaning the windshield and the grille, making adjustments to improve handling, and giving the driver a bottle of water.

Poster photograph: ©2003 CIA Stock Photography, Inc.

NASCAR

Leader of the Pack

Leader of the Pack

In NASCAR, drivers look for every edge. One way they get an edge is by "drafting," which means following the car in front of them very closely. When two or more cars running nose-to-tail, they are able to reach speeds faster than a single car.

The cars drafting behind the leader also experience less wind resistance. They are able to run more smoothly and use less fuel. Some NASCAR drivers say they actually can "feel the air" on a track to find the best and fastest way around.

Poster photograph: ©2003 Sherryl Creekmore/NASCAR

Photo Finish

NASCAR racers can reach speeds of more than 200 miles per hour! But that doesn't mean cars cross the finish line miles ahead of competitors. In fact, sometimes the difference between victory lane and a sad trip home can be the blink of an eye.

Since NASCAR started using an electronic timing system in 1993, the closest finish came in 2003 at Darlington Speedway. Ricky Craven edged Kurt Busch by two thousandths of a second! The previous record was five thousandths of a second when Dale Earnhardt Sr. snuck past Ernie Irvan at Talledega in 1993.

Poster photograph: ©2003 CIA Stock Photography, Inc.